What is Mental Health?

THE COMPLETE GUIDE

Written By Yousef Naser

Objective

Mental well-being is an intricate puzzle, a blend of biology, environment, experiences, and emotions. Every day, millions grapple with questions about their own mental health or that of their loved ones, often feeling lost amidst a whirlwind of information, misinformation, and societal judgments. "What is Mental Health?" emerges as a beacon amidst this haze, aiming to provide clarity and foster genuine understanding.

Our goal with this book is multilayered. First, we wish to equip readers with a foundation, a thorough knowledge base that demystifies the complexities of the mind. We delve into topics ranging from common disorders to the societal dimensions that impact our mental landscape. This isn't mere textbook knowledge—it's a deep dive into the world of mental health with a view to bringing the subject closer to home, making it personal, relatable, and above all, comprehensible.

Moreover, in a world rife with stigma and prejudice, there's an urgency to reshape our collective perspective on mental health. This book, therefore, also serves as an invitation—a call to foster empathy, compassion, and a more inclusive dialogue about a topic that, in one way or another, touches us all.

Why should you embark on this reading journey? Because in understanding mental health, we don't just gain knowledge; we build bridges of compassion, erode walls of ignorance, and lay the groundwork for healthier, more supportive communities. By the end of this book, "What is Mental Health?" won't just be a question—it will be an ongoing conversation, a collective commitment to wellbeing, and a testament to the importance of understanding the intricate dance of the human mind.

Come along. Every page turned is a step towards enlightenment, empathy, and empowerment. Join us in turning mental health from a whispered taboo into an open, educated, and heartfelt discussion.

Table
of Contents

Chapter 1: Introduction

Mental health remains one of the most crucial yet often misunderstood facets of human experience. At its essence, it represents the vibrant tapestry of emotions, thoughts, and social connections that underpin our daily lives. Venturing into the domain of mental health, we are presented with more than clinical definitions or the specters of disorders. Instead, we are introduced to the intricate ways through which mental health shapes our relationships, powers our achievements, and molds our perceptions of the world.

Indeed, mental health serves as the foundational bedrock of our being. From this fountainhead, we derive the strength and resilience to navigate life's varied challenges, harness our innate potentials, and become constructive members of our communities. Our mental well-being underscores our ability to make judicious decisions, cultivate rich relationships, and contribute to the socio-cultural milieu we are part of. Central to this understanding is the undeniable premise that mental health, replete with its complexities, is not just a luxury but a fundamental human right. It holds paramount importance for individual flourishing, community development, and the broader contours of socio-economic progress.

Introduction

Yet, as we delve deeper into the realm of mental health, it becomes abundantly clear that the journey transcends mere clinical diagnoses. This journey is about understanding the nuanced continuum of mental well-being that can dramatically differ from one person to another. This spectrum, with its varied shades and hues, extends beyond the binary of disorder presence or absence. It encapsulates a wide array of experiences, from the acutely distressing to the mildly perturbing, and the completely benign.

To fully grasp the scope of mental health, it becomes imperative to consider the myriad determinants that impact it. Throughout our lives, each of us navigates a labyrinth of risk and protective factors. While certain inherent psychological and biological traits might predispose some to mental health challenges, external societal dynamics, such as exposure to poverty, violence, or environmental degradation, further modulate our mental health trajectories. Notably, early childhood experiences, marked by harsh parenting or the scourge of bullying, can have indelible impacts, shaping our mental health landscape for years to come.

Yet, amidst these challenges, glimmers of hope persist. Life continually presents us with protective factors that bolster our mental resilience. These range from nurturing social interactions, quality education, fulfilling employment opportunities, to the comforting embrace of a cohesive community. Such factors, which oscillate between the micro and macro scales, intricately weave together to either uplift or erode our mental well-being.

Introduction

Acknowledging these determinants has catalyzed societal efforts to champion mental health, fostering environments that nurture mental well-being. Such endeavors transcend the traditional bounds of healthcare, permeating diverse sectors like education, housing, transportation, and environmental stewardship. Salient priorities, such as suicide prevention and the mental well-being of children and adolescents, have galvanized concerted efforts, leveraging legislative measures and ground-level interventions alike.

Moreover, while promoting mental health stands as a vital imperative, it is of equal significance to cater to those grappling with mental disorders. In recent years, the emphasis has notably shifted towards community-centric care, favoring it over traditional institutional approaches. Such a paradigm not only ensures greater accessibility but also engenders better recovery outcomes. This care spectrum encompasses everything from general health integrations to specialized mental health services and extends its reach to non-traditional settings, thereby bridging existing care gaps.

However, despite this expansive understanding, certain perennial questions persist. How does one differentiate between typical mental health and the onset of a disorder? Where does the line blur between commonplace nerves before a public speech and an entrenched mental health condition? When does ordinary shyness metamorphose into social phobia?

Introduction

Such questions beckon a nuanced understanding. Mental health is not a monolithic entity; it is the sum total of our emotional, cognitive, and behavioral wellness. A mental disorder might manifest when there's a marked disturbance in these functions, affecting various facets of life, from relationships and work to learning and daily activities. Importantly, cultural contexts and societal norms play a pivotal role in these determinations. What might be deemed ordinary in one culture could be a cause for alarm in another.

For precise diagnostics, tools like the Diagnostic and Statistical Manual of Mental Disorders (DSM) and the International Classification of Diseases (ICD) provide invaluable guidance. They offer criteria based on symptom nature, duration, and impact, elucidating the trajectory of various disorders. Health professionals, from psychiatrists to psychologists and social workers, utilize these tools, amalgamating them with personal histories, physical examinations, and other assessment methods to arrive at a conclusive diagnosis.

As we journey together through the pages of this book, we will first address the various misconceptions surrounding mental health, providing clarity and dispelling myths. We'll then delve into the most common mental health disorders, exploring their symptoms and ways of identification. The discussion will progress to treatments, shedding light on how substance abuse interacts with mental health, and investigating the role of modern technology in shaping our mental landscape.

Introduction

A more profound exploration of what constitutes mental health will ensue, leading us to examine the socio-cultural factors influencing it and providing a glimpse into the future perspectives of this domain. By the time we reach the conclusion, the aim is to present a holistic overview, facilitating a more informed, compassionate, and empathetic understanding of mental health.

Join us on this enlightening journey, as we unveil the intricate world of mental health, hoping to foster a more compassionate and understanding society for all.

Chapter 2: Misconceptions of Mental Health

In the intricate realm of mental health, shadows of misconception obscure our understanding, painting a distorted image of those who navigate its challenges.

This chapter seeks to illuminate the dense forest of myths, revealing the often-hidden realities beneath. In the intricate realm of mental health, shadows of misconception obscure our understanding, painting a distorted image of those who navigate its challenges. This chapter seeks to illuminate the dense forest of myths, revealing the often-hidden realities beneath.

For ages, misunderstandings about mental health have spread like wildfire, fueled by ignorance, societal stigmas, and ungrounded fears. It's essential to debunk these fallacies, replacing them with a framework of knowledge and compassion. For ages, misunderstandings about mental health have spread like wildfire, fueled by ignorance, societal stigmas, and ungrounded fears. It's essential to debunk these fallacies, replacing them with a framework of knowledge and compassion.

One prevalent myth suggests that mental health challenges signify weakness. However, mental health, like physical health, ebbs and flows and isn't a metric of strength. In fact, acknowledging one's challenges and seeking aid showcases immense resilience and bravery. One prevalent myth suggests that mental health challenges signify weakness. However, mental health, like physical health, ebbs and flows and isn't a metric of strength. In fact, acknowledging one's challenges and seeking aid showcases immense resilience and bravery.

Misconceptions of Mental Health

Another damaging belief is that mental health disorders are inescapable and incurable. Yet, many mental health issues, when addressed early and with appropriate interventions, can be managed. Individuals, regardless of their diagnosis, can lead fulfilling, meaningful lives. Just as physical ailments can find relief through treatments, so can mental afflictions.

Another damaging belief is that mental health disorders are inescapable and incurable. Yet, many mental health issues, when addressed early and with appropriate interventions, can be managed. Individuals, regardless of their diagnosis, can lead fulfilling, meaningful lives. Just as physical ailments can find relief through treatments, so can mental afflictions.

A particularly harmful stereotype is the association of violence with mental health issues. However, it's crucial to understand that most people with mental health challenges are not inherently violent. They are more likely to be victims rather than perpetrators. Such mischaracterizations perpetuate prejudice, constructing barriers that prevent empathy and understanding. A particularly harmful stereotype is the association of violence with mental health issues. However, it's crucial to understand that most people with mental health challenges are not inherently violent. They are more likely to be victims rather than perpetrators. Such mischaracterizations perpetuate prejudice, constructing barriers that prevent empathy and understanding.

Misconceptions wield a damaging power, influencing individual perspectives and broader societal attitudes. The stigma attached to these myths can discourage affected individuals from seeking assistance or openly discussing their experiences. This enforced silence can worsen their challenges, entrenching them in a cycle of shame and loneliness. Misconceptions wield a damaging power, influencing individual perspectives and broader societal attitudes. The stigma attached to these myths can discourage affected individuals from seeking assistance or openly discussing their experiences. This enforced silence can worsen their challenges, entrenching them in a cycle of shame and loneliness.

Misconceptions of Mental Health

On a larger scale, these misconceptions can instigate systemic discrimination, limiting the accessibility of mental health resources and further marginalizing those seeking help. On a larger scale, these misconceptions can instigate systemic discrimination, limiting the accessibility of mental health resources and further marginalizing those seeking help.

Tracing back the roots of these myths, we find a myriad of sources: ancient cultural beliefs linking mental health to supernatural forces or moral failings, exaggerated portrayals in media, and a pervasive lack of education. Tracing back the roots of these myths, we find a myriad of sources: ancient cultural beliefs linking mental health to supernatural forces or moral failings, exaggerated portrayals in media, and a pervasive lack of education.

Often, even well-meaning individuals inadvertently perpetuate these stigmatizing beliefs due to their own misunderstandings. Often, even well-meaning individuals inadvertently perpetuate these stigmatizing beliefs due to their own misunderstandings.

Education and open conversation are our strongest tools against these misconceptions. By addressing stereotypes head-on and circulating accurate information, we can cultivate a more empathetic society. Encouraging personal storytelling and fact-based discussions can shatter myths and foster understanding. Education and open conversation are our strongest tools against these misconceptions.
By addressing stereotypes head-on and circulating accurate information, we can cultivate a more empathetic society. Encouraging personal storytelling and fact-based discussions can shatter myths and foster understanding.

This quest for clarity requires a collective endeavor: governments, healthcare institutions, schools, and communities must unite to prioritize mental health care and ensure equal access to resources. This quest for clarity requires a collective endeavor: governments, healthcare institutions, schools, and communities must unite to prioritize mental health care and ensure equal access to resources.

Misconceptions of Mental Health

Now, let's address additional misconceptions to further our understanding: A frequent misbelief is that mental health issues equate to low intelligence. However, mental conditions, akin to physical ailments, can affect anyone, regardless of intelligence, social class, or financial standing. Now, let's address additional misconceptions to further our understanding: A frequent misbelief is that mental health issues equate to low intelligence. However, mental conditions, akin to physical ailments, can affect anyone, regardless of intelligence, social class, or financial standing.

Mental health care isn't exclusively for those diagnosed with a condition. Everyone benefits from nurturing their mental well-being, just as everyone benefits from physical health practices. Mental health care isn't exclusively for those diagnosed with a condition. Everyone benefits from nurturing their mental well-being, just as everyone benefits from physical health practices.

Some dismiss adolescent mental health as mere hormonal mood swings or attention-seeking behaviors. However, a significant portion of the global adolescent population grapples with mental health issues, with suicide ranking among the leading causes of death for this age group. Some dismiss adolescent mental health as mere hormonal mood swings or attention-seeking behaviors.

However, a significant portion of the global adolescent population grapples with mental health issues, with suicide ranking among the leading causes of death for this age group.

There's a fatalistic view that mental health conditions are inevitable. Yet, various protective factors can prevent their development, from strong emotional skills to supportive relationships. There's a fatalistic view that mental health conditions are inevitable. Yet, various protective factors can prevent their development, from strong emotional skills to supportive relationships.

Misconceptions of Mental Health

Associating mental health issues with weakness is another flawed notion. Recognizing and seeking help for such challenges often requires immense strength and courage. Associating mental health issues with weakness is another flawed notion. Recognizing and seeking help for such challenges often requires immense strength and courage.

The idea that adolescents with high grades and a bustling social life are immune to mental health challenges is deeply misguided. External achievements don't negate the internal emotional turmoil an individual might experience.

The idea that adolescents with high grades and a bustling social life are immune to mental health challenges is deeply misguided. External achievements don't negate the internal emotional turmoil an individual might experience.

Blaming parenting for adolescents' mental conditions oversimplifies the myriad factors influencing a young person's mental health. Blaming parenting for adolescents' mental conditions oversimplifies the myriad factors influencing a young person's mental health.

These misconceptions, among others, underline the urgency to combat stigma, share stories, and promote a broader understanding of mental health. By learning to recognize and dispel these myths, we can nurture a compassionate society that supports and uplifts all its members. These misconceptions, among others, underline the urgency to combat stigma, share stories, and promote a broader understanding of mental health. By learning to recognize and dispel these myths, we can nurture a compassionate society that supports and uplifts all its members.

Chapter 3: Most Common Mental Health Disorders

Mental health disorders, though diverse in their presentations and effects, have been an integral part of human history and experience. They are not mere medical terms or diagnoses to be relegated to clinical environments but are profound realities that many individuals confront on a daily basis. Their reach is both vast and deep, touching countless lives, regardless of race, age, gender, or socio-economic status.

The World Health Organization's data paints a telling picture, indicating that several hundred million people around the globe face challenges stemming from mental health disorders. Such statistics are not mere numbers but represent real individuals, with dreams, hopes, fears, and challenges. They are our family members, colleagues, friends, and often, they are us.

Grasping the depth and breadth of these disorders is not merely for the sake of those who suffer. It is, in fact, essential for society as a whole. When mental health is misunderstood or neglected, it does not just harm the individuals facing the disorders. The ripples of misunderstanding and neglect can stretch far and wide, affecting interpersonal relationships, workplaces, economies, and entire communities.

Yet, knowledge is the beacon that can dispel the shadows of ignorance. With understanding comes empathy, and with empathy comes a collective strength to confront and address these challenges head-on. It's more than just about medical treatments; it's about fostering an environment where stigma fades and support thrives.

In this chapter, our journey takes a closer look at some of the most common mental health disorders that people grapple with. From the profound depths of depression to the anxious pangs of generalized anxiety disorder, from the manic highs and depressive lows of bipolar disorder to the complex realities of schizophrenia - we will unravel their mysteries.

Most Common Mental Health Disorders

By exploring their causes, recognizing their symptoms, understanding treatment avenues, and hearing stories of those who live with these conditions, we aim to shed light on the very human experience behind each of these disorders.

As we navigate through these pages, our hope is to foster a deeper understanding, a stronger empathy, and a renewed commitment to addressing mental health with the seriousness and compassion it deserves. So, let us embark on this enlightening journey, where we will cover the most common mental health disorders, laying the groundwork for a world that is informed, compassionate, and proactive in its approach.

1. Depression

Depression, frequently misinterpreted as mere sadness or a transient mood swing, stands as one of the most pervasive and debilitating mental health conditions in the modern world. It delves deeper than the passing clouds of normal human emotion and anchors itself firmly in the lives of those it afflicts, casting a shadow over their daily experiences and interactions.

More than just a fleeting feeling, depression can be likened to a heavy cloak that wraps around an individual, often obscuring the colors, joys, and vibrancy of life. It doesn't lift with a good night's sleep, a chat with a friend, or even the passage of time. Unlike typical grief or sorrow, depression can persistently hover for extended periods, making days feel endless and tasks insurmountable.

Most Common Mental Health Disorders

The manifestation of depression varies considerably from one individual to another, making it a challenge to pinpoint or generalize. However, several common symptoms often serve as indicators.

These include:

1. Persistent Emotional Symptoms: Continuous feelings of sadness, hopelessness, and emptiness are hallmarks. This emotional state often disconnects individuals from their surroundings and loved ones.

2. Anhedonia: This is a technical term for the loss of interest or pleasure in activities once deemed enjoyable. Hobbies, social interactions, and even daily tasks can seem unappealing or burdensome.

3. Physical Changes: Alterations in appetite leading to significant weight gain or loss, disruptions in sleep patterns – either insomnia or hypersomnia, and an overarching sense of fatigue or lethargy.

4. Cognitive Impairments: These include challenges in concentrating, thinking clearly, or making decisions. A once clear mind might feel fogged or distant.

5. Heightened Self-Criticism: Persistent feelings of worthlessness or excessive guilt, often over minor matters or past mistakes.

6. Dark Thoughts: In severe cases, recurrent thoughts of death, self-harm, or suicide can emerge, indicating an urgent need for intervention and support.

Most Common Mental Health Disorders

The causes of depression are multifaceted and intertwined, creating a unique tapestry for each person. Some individuals have a genetic predisposition, making them more susceptible. For others, neurotransmitter imbalances in the brain or hormonal changes play significant roles. Traumatic life events, chronic stress, or even prolonged isolation can serve as triggers. Environmental factors, such as the loss of a loved one, financial troubles, or significant life changes, also contribute. Additionally, underlying medical conditions or medications can induce depressive symptoms.

When it comes to addressing depression, a personalized approach is paramount. For many, a combination of psychotherapy (or talk therapy) and medications proves effective. Cognitive Behavioral Therapy (CBT), for instance, equips individuals with tools to reframe negative thought patterns. Antidepressant medications can assist in balancing brain chemicals. Alongside these, lifestyle adjustments such as regular physical activity, a balanced diet, adequate sleep, stress-reduction techniques, and strong social support can significantly bolster recovery.

Understanding depression requires more than just recognizing its clinical facets. It involves acknowledging the profound human experience of those navigating its tumultuous waters and reinforcing the essential message that with the right support, resilience is possible, and healing is within reach.

Most Common Mental Health Disorders

2. Anxiety Disorders

Anxiety Disorders: While fleeting moments of anxiety are universal and woven into the fabric of life's experiences, anxiety disorders exist in a realm far beyond this normalcy. These disorders engulf individuals in an atmosphere of intense, excessive, and persistent dread and apprehension about routine situations, overshadowing the simplicity of daily life.

 Distinctively, many also experience panic attacks – alarming bouts of overpowering fear that crescendo rapidly, often peaking within mere minutes. These episodes and feelings don't merely dissipate; they cascade into one's daily existence, complicating tasks, morphing perceptions, and frequently leading to avoidance behaviors, all in an attempt to evade these overpowering emotions. The onset can trace back to formative years, casting a shadow that may stretch into adulthood.

Generalized Anxiety Disorder (GAD): Magnified Worry in Mundane Moments

Among the spectrum of anxiety disorders, Generalized Anxiety Disorder or GAD stands uniquely with its overarching concerns about everyday activities and events. It isn't merely about feeling anxious; it's the magnification of worry, often out of sync with the actual scenario, making it difficult to manage. It's like viewing life through a lens that distorts the scale of challenges, and it's frequently accompanied by physical symptoms.

The unease isn't confined to the mind; it manifests physically, with indications ranging from palpitations and hyperventilation to gastrointestinal issues and fatigue. Notably, GAD often doesn't exist in isolation; its presence can intertwine with other anxiety disorders or even depression.

Most Common Mental Health Disorders

Panic Disorder: The Unpredictable Onset of Intense Fear

Panic Disorder captures the essence of unpredictability in the realm of anxiety disorders. It's characterized by recurrent episodes of intense anxiety, or panic attacks, that ascend rapidly, often without forewarning. The symptoms are unmistakable: a sensation of looming doom, difficulty in breathing, heart palpitations, and even chest pain. Following these episodes, the residual fear – of their recurrence and the associated situations – can be paralyzing.

A Broad Spectrum of Anxiety Disorders. The landscape of anxiety disorders is vast:

• Agoraphobia: This disorder magnifies the fear of places or situations that might induce panic, rendering individuals feeling trapped or embarrassed.

• Anxiety due to Medical Conditions: Here, physical health issues directly trigger symptoms of overwhelming anxiety.

• Selective Mutism: Predominantly observed in children, it's marked by their inability to speak in specific situations, even though they can articulate in others.

• Separation Anxiety Disorder: Children exhibit excessive anxiety beyond their developmental stage, especially when separated from parental figures.

• Social Anxiety Disorder: Individuals experience high anxiety levels in social situations, fearing judgment, embarrassment, or negative perceptions.

• Specific Phobias: Exposure to particular objects or situations induces severe anxiety, sometimes culminating in panic attacks.

• Substance-induced Anxiety Disorder: This is a resultant of drug misuse, certain medications, toxic exposures, or even withdrawal symptoms.

Other Specified & Unspecified Anxiety Disorders: These encapsulate anxieties or phobias that don't align entirely with the specified categories but are significant in their impact.

Most Common Mental Health Disorders

<u>3. Attention-Deficit/Hyperactivity Disorder (ADHD)</u>

Attention-Deficit/Hyperactivity Disorder, commonly known as ADHD, is a widespread neurodevelopmental disorder that predominantly emerges during childhood. Manifesting as persistent patterns of inattention, hyperactivity, and impulsivity, the disorder varies in its presentation among individuals. Some might predominantly show symptoms of inattention, while others may exhibit more hyperactive and impulsive behaviors. Still, others may have a combination of both.

Children and ADHD: For children diagnosed with ADHD, everyday tasks that seem routine for their peers become monumental challenges. From focusing in class and completing assignments to listening to instructions at home, the effects of ADHD can permeate all aspects of a child's life. This often results in academic struggles, leading to frustration and a subsequent decline in self-esteem. Furthermore, their impulsive behavior can interfere with social interactions, leading them to be misunderstood by peers and even leading to potential feelings of isolation.

ADHD in Adulthood: While many consider ADHD to be a childhood disorder, its implications often stretch well into adulthood. Adults with ADHD might struggle with organizational tasks, time management, and maintaining steady employment. Their relationships might be strained due to forgetfulness, impulsive decisions, or a perceived lack of responsibility. It's not uncommon for adults with undiagnosed ADHD to feel restless and unable to find a structured path in life.

Root Causes and Contributing Factors: While the exact origin of ADHD remains elusive, various factors contribute to its development. Genetics appears to play a pivotal role, with the disorder often running in families. Environmental factors, such as exposure to certain toxins during pregnancy, premature birth, and low birth weight, may also heighten the risk. Brain injuries, especially those affecting the frontal lobe which governs decision-making and impulse control, have been linked to ADHD-like symptoms.

Most Common Mental Health Disorders

Holistic Treatment Approaches: Addressing ADHD requires a comprehensive, multifaceted approach tailored to each individual's unique needs.

1. Medication: Predominantly stimulants, these drugs aim to balance and enhance neurotransmitter activity in the brain. While they can significantly improve concentration and control impulsivity, they come with potential side effects, necessitating close monitoring by a healthcare professional.

2. Psychotherapy: Cognitive-behavioral therapy (CBT) can equip individuals with ADHD with strategies to manage their symptoms, improve self-esteem, and enhance their interpersonal skills.

3. Educational Interventions: Structured education and training sessions can provide children and adults with practical techniques to handle daily challenges, from classroom settings to workplace scenarios.

4. Lifestyle Changes: A balanced diet, rich in essential nutrients, can positively influence brain function. Regular exercise has been found to enhance focus and reduce impulsivity. Adequate sleep is crucial, as fatigue can exacerbate ADHD symptoms.

5. Support Groups: Sharing experiences and coping techniques with others facing similar challenges can offer a vital sense of community and understanding.

6. Alternative Therapies: Some families have found benefits in biofeedback, meditation, and certain dietary interventions, though it's essential to consult with professionals before considering these options.

With early diagnosis, consistent support, and an individualized treatment plan, individuals with ADHD can channel their unique strengths, overcome associated challenges, and lead fulfilling lives.

Most Common Mental Health Disorders

4. Bipolar Disorder

Bipolar disorder, formerly termed manic-depressive illness, is a mental health condition characterized by intense and unpredictable shifts in mood, energy, activity, and concentration. These swings aren't merely the regular emotional fluctuations most people experience; they are so profound that they can disrupt daily life.

The disorder has several variations. Bipolar I Disorder manifests as intense manic episodes lasting for a week or requiring immediate medical intervention due to their severity. These manic phases often alternate with depressive episodes that last for at least two weeks. In some cases, individuals with Bipolar I encounter mixed episodes, where both manic and depressive symptoms occur simultaneously. If they experience four or more such episodes within a year, this is known as "rapid cycling."

Bipolar II Disorder encompasses patterns of depressive episodes interwoven with less severe manic episodes, termed hypomania. Another variation is Cyclothymic Disorder, or Cyclothymia, which is marked by periodic, mild manic and depressive symptoms that don't reach the full intensity of typical manic or depressive episodes. Beyond these types, some bipolar symptoms don't fit neatly into these categories, leading to a diagnosis of "other specified and unspecified bipolar and related disorders."

Individuals with bipolar disorder experience periods of extreme emotions, disrupted sleep patterns, varying activity levels, and often demonstrate behaviors that markedly deviate from their usual selves. These episodes can be so distinct that friends and family can recognize these shifts as warning signs, even if the individual perceives them as productive periods, particularly in states of hypomania.

Most Common Mental Health Disorders

The process of diagnosing bipolar disorder is intricate. It generally starts with a health care provider's assessment and may proceed to a comprehensive mental health evaluation. The diagnosis hinges on personal symptoms, life experiences, and occasionally, family medical history. This becomes especially vital in younger individuals.

An essential aspect of understanding bipolar disorder is acknowledging its potential coexistence with other conditions. It can co-occur with anxiety disorders, ADHD, substance misuse, and eating disorders. Severe manic or depressive episodes can even present psychotic symptoms like hallucinations or delusions, often aligning with the mood episode's nature.

Though the precise causes of bipolar disorder are still under exploration, differences in brain structures and functionality might be contributing factors. Genetics also play a role, with certain genes potentially heightening susceptibility, especially if there's a family history.

The treatment for bipolar disorder is diverse. Medications, notably mood stabilizers such as lithium, valproic acid, and lamotrigine, are common therapeutic tools. Antipsychotics might be added if manic or depressive symptoms persist despite other treatments. In some cases, antipsychotics may be used in conjunction with mood stabilizers. Antidepressants can also be administered, but they're typically paired with a mood stabilizer or antipsychotic to prevent potential manic episodes. Benzodiazepines might be employed on a short-term basis to alleviate anxiety and improve sleep.

The medication journey often requires experimentation to determine the most effective drug and dose for an individual. This process requires patience, as many medications take weeks or even months to demonstrate their full impact. Furthermore, side effects, though often temporary, can be a concern, making it crucial for individuals to communicate with their healthcare providers and never alter or stop medication without professional guidance.

Most Common Mental Health Disorders

Pregnancy introduces another dimension to treatment, as some bipolar disorder medications can lead to birth defects and can be transferred to the baby through breast milk. Therefore, it's imperative to discuss treatment options with a doctor if pregnancy is planned or suspected.

Beyond medications, psychotherapy plays a pivotal role in treating bipolar disorder. Techniques such as Interpersonal and Social Rhythm Therapy (IPSRT), Cognitive Behavioral Therapy (CBT), and family-focused therapy offer various tools to manage the disorder. They help in establishing routines, developing coping mechanisms, understanding the disorder, and strengthening familial bonds.

Other treatments like electroconvulsive therapy (ECT) and transcranial magnetic stimulation (TMS) might be considered for those who don't respond to conventional treatments. ECT involves passing electrical currents through the brain to induce a brief seizure, leading to changes in brain chemistry that can alleviate certain mental illness symptoms. TMS is still under research as a potential treatment option.

When it comes to children and teenagers, treatments are often tailored according to the individual's symptoms, medication side effects, and other factors. As with adults, a combination of medication and psychotherapy is generally pursued, emphasizing the importance of a structured routine, coping skills, and family support.

In essence, the treatment of bipolar disorder is comprehensive, blending medication, therapy, and lifestyle adjustments to aid individuals in managing their condition effectively.

Most Common Mental Health Disorders

5. Schizophrenia

Schizophrenia is a complex and often misunderstood mental health disorder that impacts an individual's ability to think clearly, manage emotions, and relate to others. Its symptoms can be categorized into three primary areas: positive symptoms, negative symptoms, and cognitive symptoms. Positive symptoms involve distortions of normal functions, such as hallucinations, delusions, and thought disorders. Negative symptoms include a reduction in normal functions, such as limited speech productivity, decreased ability to experience pleasure, lack of motivation, and limited emotional expression. Cognitive symptoms encompass problems with thought processes, like impaired attention, poor executive functioning, and trouble with working memory.

The causes of schizophrenia are multifaceted, involving genetic predispositions, brain chemistry, environmental factors, and substance use. A person's likelihood of developing schizophrenia rises if a close family member has the condition, and certain neurotransmitters, like dopamine and glutamate, may also play a role. Environmental factors like stressful events, viral infections during infancy, or maternal gestation can contribute to the onset, and substances like marijuana, LSD, or methamphetamines might exacerbate the condition in predisposed individuals.

Treatment for schizophrenia often requires a combination of medical, psychological, and social interventions. Antipsychotic medications, such as risperidone, olanzapine, and aripiprazole, are often used to influence dopamine levels in the brain and are effective in treating positive symptoms. However, negative symptoms can prove more resistant. Alongside medications, psychotherapy plays a crucial role. Cognitive Behavioral Therapy (CBT) helps patients identify and modify distorted thought patterns and beliefs, supportive therapy improves daily living skills, and family therapy provides essential support to families.

Most Common Mental Health Disorders

In more severe cases, hospitalization may be necessary to provide a safe environment to stabilize acute symptoms. Electroconvulsive Therapy (ECT) might also be considered for individuals who don't respond to traditional therapies, especially if they are also experiencing severe depression. Rehabilitation programs, including job counseling, problem-solving support, and social skills training, help integrate those with schizophrenia more successfully into their communities. Additionally, support groups can provide emotional and practical support by connecting patients and families with others who share similar experiences.

While schizophrenia remains a chronic condition, the combination of these treatment strategies can enable many affected individuals to lead rewarding and meaningful lives. Effective management is tailored to the individual, addressing their unique symptoms and needs, and often requires a collaborative effort from medical professionals, therapists, family members, and the individuals themselves.

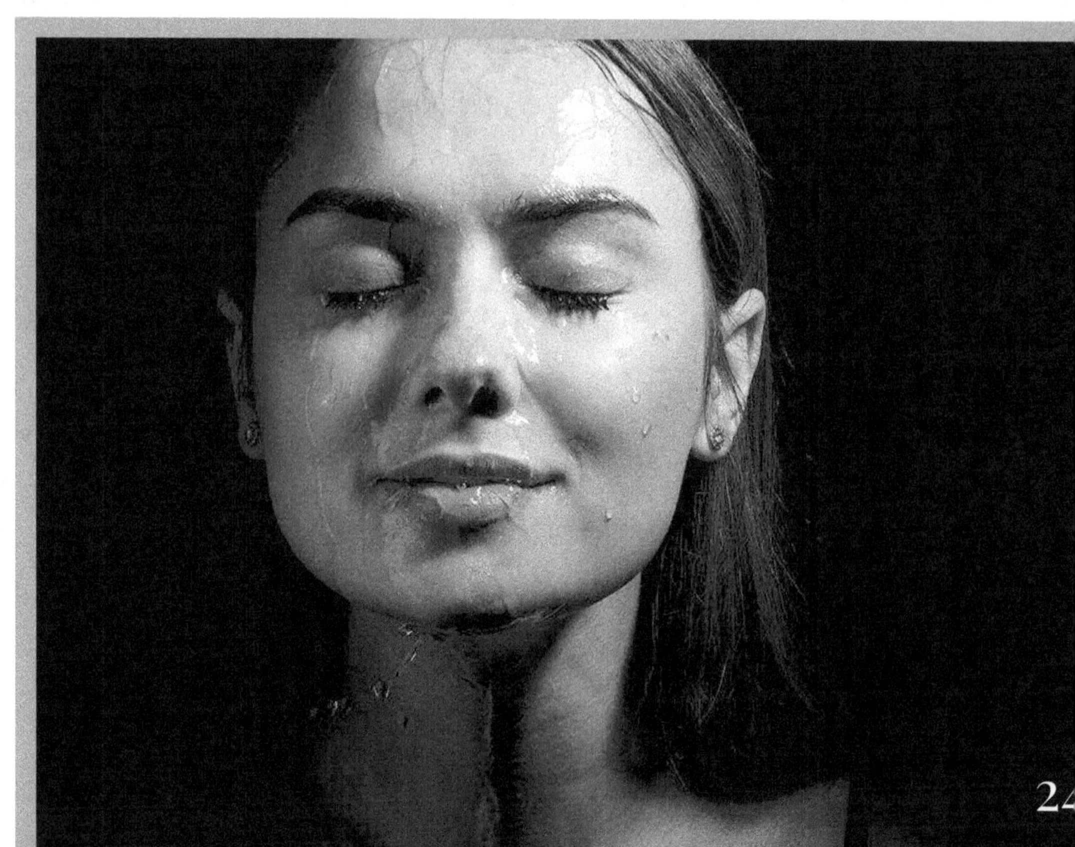

Most Common Mental Health Disorders

6. Personality Disorders

Personality disorders encapsulate a spectrum of mental health conditions, hallmarked by rigid and maladaptive patterns of thinking, feeling, and behaving. Unlike temporary behavioral responses to stressful events, these ingrained patterns persist across various situations and can significantly interfere with personal, social, and professional relationships.

The intricate mosaic of personality disorders includes diverse classifications. For instance, individuals with borderline personality disorder frequently grapple with intense emotional swings, unstable relationships, and a wavering self-image. Antisocial personality disorder is characterized by a persistent pattern of disregard for others' rights, often crossing into violations. Those with narcissistic personality disorder tend to exhibit an inflated sense of their own importance, a profound need for admiration, and a lack of empathy, often masking fragile self-esteem vulnerable to the slightest criticism.

What is particularly poignant about these conditions is the individual's perception of the world and themselves. Many times, people with personality disorders maintain a distorted self-image. Their behavior, no matter how out of sync with reality or social norms, might seem entirely rational and justified to them. This self-perception can complicate their relationships, as they might not recognize their role in interpersonal conflicts and instead attribute them entirely to others.

Most Common Mental Health Disorders

The treatment landscape for personality disorders emphasizes psychological therapies tailored to the specific disorder and its severity. Structured therapy sessions are paramount. Cognitive Behavioral Therapy (CBT) is often employed to challenge and reshape distorted thoughts and behaviors while promoting healthier coping mechanisms. Dialectical Behavior Therapy (DBT), particularly effective for borderline personality disorder, merges cognitive-based approaches with mindfulness strategies.

It aids in emotional regulation, interpersonal effectiveness, and distress tolerance. Schema-focused therapy delves into identifying and changing negative beliefs about oneself, while psychodynamic psychotherapy seeks to resolve unconscious conflicts rooted in childhood.

Additionally, medications may be prescribed to treat associated symptoms or conditions, such as depression or anxiety, rather than the personality disorder itself. It's important to note that treatment success hinges on the recognition of the disorder and a genuine desire to change, often necessitating long-term therapeutic involvement.

Through consistent therapeutic intervention, individuals can achieve a better understanding of themselves, cultivate healthier interpersonal skills, and foster improved life quality.

Most Common Mental Health Disorders

7. Eating Disorders

Eating disorders epitomize a complex interplay of mental and physical health challenges, underlined by profoundly distorted perceptions of body image and self-worth. These disorders do not merely focus on food but pivot around deep-seated emotions, attitudes, and obsessions. The ramifications extend beyond psychological distress, often manifesting as severe physical health complications.

At the forefront of these conditions is Anorexia Nervosa, a disorder steeped in an overwhelming dread of weight gain. This fear becomes so overarching that individuals drastically limit their food intake, irrespective of their actual body weight. Alarmingly, those grappling with anorexia may perceive themselves as overweight, even when their body is emaciated.

The health complications arising from this self-imposed starvation are myriad, ranging from cardiovascular issues to bone density loss, and tragically, anorexia claims more lives than any other mental health disorder. The blend of physical deterioration with the emotional toll exacerbates the risk of suicide.

In contrast, Bulimia Nervosa is punctuated by cyclical episodes. Individuals might consume an unusually large amount of food in a short duration, only to be consumed by guilt and resort to extreme measures to counteract the potential weight gain. These compensatory behaviors can take the form of induced vomiting, over-exercising, or misuse of laxatives. Despite these apparent differences from anorexia, the underlying psyche is eerily similar; a looming anxiety about weight gain and an acute dissatisfaction with one's body.

Most Common Mental Health Disorders

Shifting the focus to Binge-Eating Disorder, one observes a different dynamic. While it stands as the most prevalent eating disorder in the U.S., it differentiates itself from bulimia in one key aspect: the absence of regular compensatory behaviors. Individuals consume excessive quantities of food, often in secrecy, without subsequent episodes of purging or extreme exercise. The emotional aftermath is a cocktail of guilt, shame, and distress.

Navigating the path to recovery from eating disorders necessitates a multifaceted approach. A combination of psychological counseling, nutritional education, and medical monitoring proves most effective. Cognitive Behavioral Therapy (CBT) is frequently employed, assisting individuals in identifying negative thought patterns and developing healthier coping strategies.

Some might benefit from medications, particularly to address accompanying anxiety or depression. Furthermore, group therapy or support groups can be instrumental, offering a platform for shared experiences, understanding, and mutual encouragement. Crucially, early intervention and a tailored treatment plan enhance the likelihood of recovery, steering individuals towards a healthier relationship with food and self-image.

Most Common Mental Health Disorders

8. Addictions

Addiction, a deeply rooted and multifaceted condition, presents itself in various forms, ensnaring individuals in a relentless cycle of cravings, compulsions, and continual engagement. The world of addiction encompasses a wide range of both substances and behaviors, from the tangible like drugs and alcohol to the intangible like habits and compulsions.

Substance addiction remains a prime concern. These are typically dependencies on physical substances, which when ingested, can cause a debilitating dependency. The frequent narrative sees an individual starting off with casual or recreational usage, which spirals into a full-fledged addiction. This could involve legal substances like alcohol or prescription drugs, or illegal substances that not only modify one's perception temporarily but might induce irreversible damage to vital organs and the brain, especially if abused over time.

Then, we drift into the realm of behavioral addictions. Sex addiction, for instance, is not about the act itself but the compulsive need for the neurochemical thrill it offers. Food addiction is another behavioral pattern where individuals might find comfort or escape in eating, often irrespective of hunger cues.

In our digital age, social media addiction has surfaced as a real concern, with platforms like Instagram or Facebook crafting experiences that stimulate our brain's reward centers, sometimes as intensely as certain drugs might. Similarly, pornography addiction stands out, where individuals become reliant on explicit content, often affecting their real-world relationships and self-perception.

Most Common Mental Health Disorders

Beyond these, there are other behavioral compulsions like the addiction to exercise, which might sound beneficial but can be detrimental when overdone, leading to physical injury or an unhealthy obsession. Working addiction, colloquially known as 'workaholism,' sees individuals incessantly immersed in their job or profession, often at the cost of personal relationships and health. Spiritual obsession might involve excessive indulgence in religious or spiritual practices to the point where it disrupts daily life. The addiction to cutting or self-harm is a more harrowing form of addiction where individuals inflict pain upon themselves as a coping mechanism. Lastly, the world of video gaming, while a source of entertainment for many, can transform into an addiction for some, leading to hours spent in virtual realms and often neglecting real-world responsibilities.

Irrespective of the type, the repercussions of any addiction can be severe. Continuous indulgence can modify the brain's functions, hampering decision-making, memory, learning, and judgment. Over time, the physical and mental health ramifications can be enormous, from organ damage and susceptibility to diseases to strained personal relationships and potential legal or financial issues.

Yet, in this often overwhelming landscape of addiction, there exists hope and the promise of recovery. Both substance and behavioral addictions can be addressed effectively. Tailored treatment plans, focusing on the specifics of each addiction, can guide individuals back to a balanced life. These interventions can range from medical treatment and rehab programs to therapy and support groups.

A blend of behavioral therapies, medication, structured routines, and community support can pave the way for a renewed, fulfilling life. For those grappling with any form of addiction, it's crucial to recognize the issue and seek professional assistance, ensuring a brighter, healthier future.

Most Common Mental Health Disorders

Treatment for addiction is multifaceted, aiming not just to address the physical aspect of dependency but also the psychological factors that contribute to it. Hospital management is a pivotal component, especially for those withdrawing from certain substances that pose severe health risks. Specialized hospital units are equipped to offer intensive monitoring and therapeutic interventions, ensuring that individuals are safely supported as they navigate the challenging terrain of withdrawal.

Another instrumental treatment option is the use of medications. Some are specifically designed to curb cravings, suppress urges, and mitigate the effects of prolonged withdrawal. Additionally, if an individual with addiction also struggles with other mental health disorders, such as depression or bipolar disorder, healthcare providers might prescribe medications to manage those conditions concurrently. This holistic approach ensures that all interlinked issues are addressed, maximizing the chances of sustained recovery.

Rehabilitation, often referred to as rehab, offers a structured environment for recovery, whether it be a residential setting (inpatient rehab) or through scheduled sessions at a facility (outpatient rehab).

Rehab centers prioritize structured counseling, education, and support, creating a conducive atmosphere for individuals to learn, grow, and equip themselves with the skills needed to combat addiction in the long run.

The primary objective is to instill habits and knowledge that enable individuals to lead healthier, addiction-free lives.

Most Common Mental Health Disorders

Therapy plays an indispensable role in addiction treatment. Through various forms of psychotherapy, individuals gain insights into the root causes of their addiction, learn coping mechanisms, and develop strategies to prevent relapse.

Techniques such as cognitive behavioral therapy can be particularly effective, as they delve into the cognitive patterns that fuel addiction and work towards reshaping them. Group therapy, on the other hand, offers a communal space for individuals to share, relate, and heal together.

Lastly, support groups serve as a lifeline for many battling addiction. Organizations like Alcoholics Anonymous or Narcotics Anonymous have garnered worldwide recognition for their role in helping individuals sustain recovery.

These groups offer a sense of community, understanding, and shared purpose. For the families and friends of those struggling with substance use disorders, groups such as Al-Anon provide solace and guidance. By sharing experiences and offering mutual support, these groups act as a cornerstone in the lifelong journey of recovery.

In essence, the path to overcoming addiction requires a comprehensive approach, integrating medical, psychological, and communal support. With the right combination of treatments, countless individuals have reclaimed their lives from the grasp of addiction, underscoring the importance and effectiveness of these interventions.

Most Common Mental Health Disorders

9. Post-Traumatic Stress Disorder (PTSD)

Post-Traumatic Stress Disorder, commonly referred to as PTSD, is a debilitating mental health condition that emerges in the aftermath of a traumatic event. Such events can range from violent personal encounters, natural disasters, severe accidents, to the harrowing experiences of warfare. Individuals with PTSD find themselves trapped in the distressing memories of the trauma, often reliving them through intense flashbacks or haunting nightmares. These vivid recollections can disrupt daily life, making it immensely challenging for sufferers to move past the incident.

The repercussions of PTSD are not confined to intrusive memories alone. A pervasive sense of severe anxiety accompanies these memories, casting a shadow over every facet of an individual's life. This heightened state of alertness, often termed as hyperarousal, can manifest in varied ways, including difficulty sleeping, irritability, and an exaggerated startle response.

Moreover, individuals might find themselves persistently avoiding reminders of the traumatic event, leading to social withdrawal and a profound sense of emotional numbness.

Intrusive thoughts about the traumatic event are another hallmark of PTSD. These thoughts can be incessant and overwhelmingly distressing, causing a person to feel as if they are perpetually ensnared in the traumatic moment. The mental replay can trigger intense emotional and physical reactions, making it difficult for the person to distinguish between past traumas and present realities.

Most Common Mental Health Disorders

Addressing PTSD necessitates a multifaceted approach. Therapy is one of the cornerstone treatments for this condition. Cognitive Behavioral Therapy (CBT), for instance, equips individuals with skills to reframe negative thought patterns and confront their fears in a safe environment. Exposure therapy, a subset of CBT, can also be effective by allowing individuals to face and control their memories of the traumatic event.

On the pharmaceutical front, certain medications have proven efficacious in managing symptoms. Antidepressants can be particularly beneficial in alleviating the depressive and anxiety symptoms associated with PTSD.

Moreover, Eye Movement Desensitization and Reprocessing (EMDR) has emerged as a promising technique in recent years. It involves guiding patients in making specific eye movements while recalling traumatic events, which can aid in processing and integrating traumatic memories.

The journey to recovery from PTSD can be long and arduous, but with the right combination of therapeutic interventions and medications, many individuals find their path to healing. Crucially, seeking timely and professional help is of paramount importance, ensuring that those afflicted can rebuild their lives with resilience and hope.

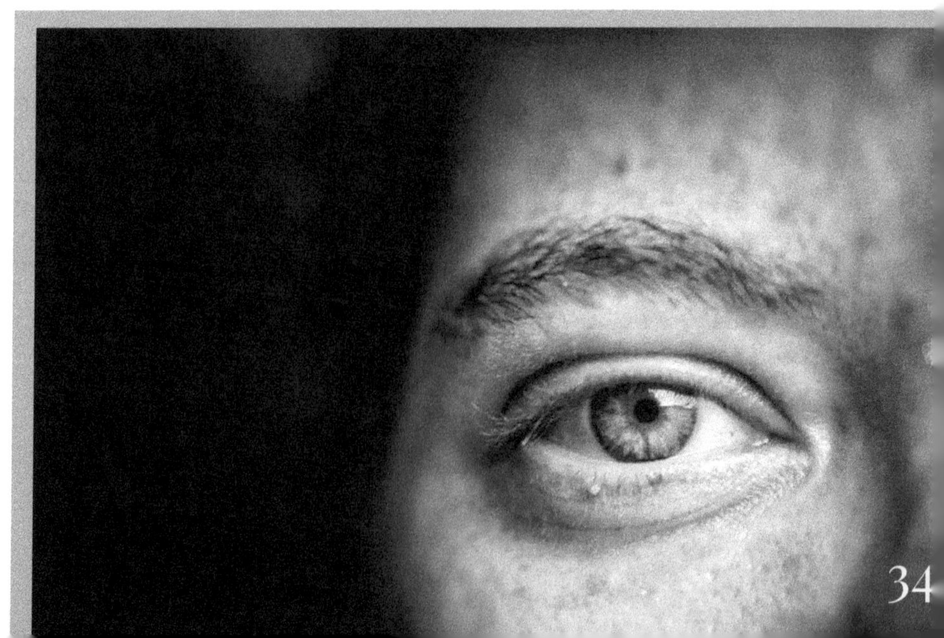

Most Common Mental Health Disorders

11. Obsessive-Compulsive Disorder (OCD)

Obsessive-Compulsive Disorder, commonly known as OCD, is a nuanced mental health disorder characterized by the interplay of persistent, unwelcome thoughts (obsessions) and repetitive behaviors or mental rituals (compulsions). Unlike transient worries or everyday habits, these obsessions are all-consuming, often dictating substantial parts of a person's day and detrimentally affecting their overall well-being.

At the heart of OCD lie these obsessions—recurrent and intrusive thoughts, images, or urges that provoke intense feelings of anxiety or revulsion. T

o alleviate the distress stirred by these obsessions, individuals with OCD resort to specific behaviors or mental acts, the compulsions. For instance, a person tormented by the recurring fear of germs might wash their hands excessively, even if rationally, they recognize the redundancy of such actions.

It's essential to debunk the common misconceptions surrounding OCD. It isn't just about a desire for orderliness or a penchant for cleanliness. Instead, it's a crippling ailment driven by profound anxiety or fear.

People with OCD don't indulge in compulsive behaviors for joy or out of mere preference. They're trapped in these routines, seeking temporary relief from the intense distress caused by their obsessions. Unfortunately, this solace is fleeting, dragging them back into the unforgiving loop of their compulsions time and again.

Most Common Mental Health Disorders

Acknowledging the profound toll OCD can exact on someone's daily life and emotional health, the silver lining is the existence of effective therapeutic approaches. Among the most potent treatments for OCD is Cognitive Behavioral Therapy (CBT), especially its specialized form, Exposure and Response Prevention (ERP). In ERP, individuals confront their obsessive fears in a controlled environment and are discouraged from resorting to their compulsive behaviors. Over time, this method diminishes the anxiety associated with their obsessions. Medicinally, a particular group of drugs known as Selective Serotonin Reuptake Inhibitors (SSRIs) has shown promise in alleviating OCD symptoms, complementing therapeutic interventions.

To encapsulate, OCD, with its unique challenges, can indeed cast a long shadow over one's life. However, armed with the right knowledge, timely diagnosis, and strategic treatments, those affected can transcend these challenges, breaking free from the fetters of their obsessions and compulsions. In doing so, they pave the way for a life abundant in meaning, contentment, and joy.

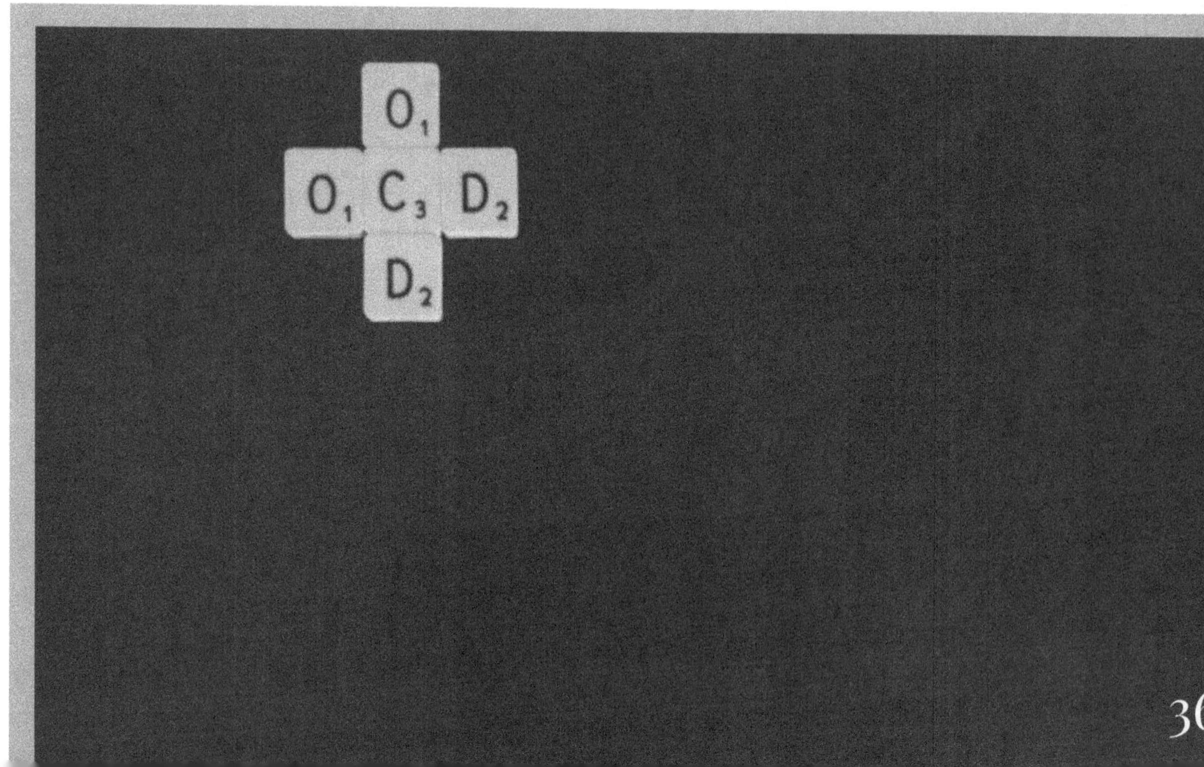

Chapter 4: Symptoms & Identification

Navigating the labyrinth of our own mind can be intricate and challenging. Often, there's a thin line between what we perceive as 'just a phase' and what might be an indication of a deeper mental health issue. Recognizing and understanding these signs is the first pivotal step towards seeking help or assisting someone in need.

General Signs of Mental Health Disorders

Every mental health disorder possesses its own distinct set of symptoms. However, there are overarching signs that might indicate that someone is grappling with a mental health challenge:

1. Persistent Sadness or Irritability: It's natural to have days when we feel down. However, a continuous feeling of sadness or irritability that doesn't seem to abate could be a sign of a deeper issue.

2. Extreme Mood Fluctuations: Dramatic swings between emotional highs and lows that affect one's daily functioning could be indicative of mood disorders.

3. Withdrawal: A stark change in social activities, avoiding friends, or retreating into a shell can often be a clear sign of distress.

4. Drastic Changes in Appetite and Sleep Patterns: Overeating, not eating enough, insomnia, or oversleeping might be more than just passing phases.

5. Unexplained Physical Ailments: Often, our mental and emotional state can manifest physically in the form of headaches, back pains, or stomach issues.

Symptoms & Identification

6. Confusion or Decreased Ability to Concentrate: A sudden struggle with concentration, decision-making, or a feeling of perpetual 'fog' could be a signal.

7. Feeling Overwhelmed or Hopeless: An intense feeling of despair or thinking there's no way out of situations is a sign that shouldn't be ignored.

8. Increased Sensitivity: Heightened sensitivity to sights, sounds, smells or touch; avoidance of over-stimulating situations.

9. Apathy: Losing interest in previously cherished activities or feeling indifferent towards significant events can be revealing.

10. Excessive Fears or Worries: Persistent fears or worries that seem disproportionate to the situation at hand.

11. Substance Abuse: An increased reliance on drugs, alcohol, or other substances can often be an attempt to self-medicate or escape from underlying issues.

12. Multiple Physical Complaints: Frequent visits to health care providers, despite the absence of a physical cause, can sometimes be a cry for help.

13. Thinking About Death or Suicide: Suicidal thoughts or gestures always require immediate attention and intervention.

Symptoms & Identification

Importance of Professional Diagnosis

While the above signs can serve as red flags, self-diagnosis or diagnosing others without professional intervention can be fraught with danger. Here's why:

1. Complexity of Mental Health Disorders: The nuances of each disorder are intricate, often overlapping, making it challenging to pinpoint a specific issue without a thorough assessment.

2. Risk of Misdiagnosis: Without a structured, professional diagnostic process, there's a risk of either overlooking a critical issue or misidentifying it altogether.

3. Professional Expertise: Mental health professionals are trained to evaluate symptoms in the context of an individual's life, history, and the broader spectrum of mental health.

4. Tailored Treatment Plans: A correct diagnosis paves the way for a tailored treatment plan, ensuring the individual receives the most effective therapeutic interventions.

5. Avoiding Self-Stigmatization: Labeling oneself without a proper diagnosis can lead to unnecessary self-stigmatization or might create barriers to seeking appropriate help.

6. Holistic Understanding: A professional can offer a holistic understanding, considering biological, psychological, and social factors in their diagnosis.

In essence, while recognizing symptoms is a crucial step in the right direction, seeking a professional opinion ensures that one treads this complex journey with clarity, understanding, and the right support. It's imperative to remember that mental health is just as critical as physical health, requiring the same diligence, care, and expertise.

Chapter 5: Treatments

The journey towards mental wellness often involves a combination of therapies and interventions. When addressing mental health disorders, the type and severity of the condition, individual preferences, and other personal factors play a pivotal role in dictating the treatment pathway. In this chapter, we will delve into the multifaceted world of treatments that have emerged and evolved over time, offering solace to countless individuals.

Psychotherapy

Often termed 'talk therapy,' psychotherapy is more than just talking about your problems. Rooted in dialogues, this therapeutic approach allows an individual to delve into their feelings, beliefs, and behaviors, facilitated by a trained therapist. It provides a confidential, empathetic space for individuals to understand and confront their psychological challenges.

Over sessions that might span weeks, months, or even years, individuals often uncover deeper layers of themselves. While the initial conversations might revolve around current life events or issues, subsequent sessions might uncover patterns or past events that influence present behaviors. By understanding these patterns, individuals can often find ways to make changes and live a more fulfilling life.

Cognitive Behavioral Therapy (CBT)

CBT stands apart due to its structured, problem-focused approach. It's not merely about understanding one's feelings but more about learning tools to tackle negative thought patterns head-on.

During CBT sessions, individuals are encouraged to explore the relationship between thoughts, feelings, and behaviors. A person might be asked to challenge certain ingrained beliefs or confront and reframe automatic negative thoughts. By doing so, they can often modify maladaptive behaviors and reactions. For instance, someone with social anxiety might start recognizing that not all social events lead to negative outcomes, thereby gradually reducing their avoidance behavior.

Treatments

Dialectical Behavior Therapy (DBT)

Initially conceptualized for treating borderline personality disorder, DBT brings together cognitive-behavioral approaches with eastern meditative practices. A highlight of DBT is its focus on acceptance and change. Individuals are taught skills to accept their experiences while also learning strategies to change negative patterns.

DBT often involves both group and individual sessions. The group sessions emphasize skill-building, while individual sessions focus on personal challenges and applying these skills in real-world scenarios. Skills are categorized into four modules: mindfulness, interpersonal effectiveness, distress tolerance, and emotion regulation.

Psychoanalytic Therapy

A dive into the depths of the unconscious mind, psychoanalytic therapy, is a journey back in time. Drawing heavily from Freud's theories, this therapy believes that unresolved childhood conflicts influence current behaviors.

Patients and therapists spend hours discussing dreams, past memories, and daily life, looking for symbolic meanings and hidden patterns. By uncovering these buried memories and understanding them, individuals can often release pent-up emotions and experience relief from their symptoms.

Treatments

Medications and Their Side Effects

Medications have revolutionized the treatment of several mental health disorders, offering symptomatic relief and improving the quality of life. Depending on the disorder in question, psychiatrists might prescribe antidepressants, antipsychotics, mood stabilizers, or anti-anxiety drugs.

However, these medications aren't without their challenges. Side effects are common, ranging from mild nuisances like dry mouth or dizziness to more concerning issues like weight gain or a blunting of emotions. Additionally, there's often a trial and error involved in finding the right medication and dosage. Regular consultations with a psychiatrist are crucial to monitor progress and adjust treatment as necessary.

Home Remedies

While clinical treatments remain foundational, there's a lot one can do within the confines of their home to supplement their mental health journey. Activities like regular exercise can stimulate the brain's release of endorphins, boosting mood. A diet replete with omega-3 fatty acids, antioxidants, and essential vitamins can potentially nurture brain health.

Mindfulness practices, including meditation and yoga, have been found to reduce symptoms of anxiety and depression for some individuals. They promote a state of awareness and acceptance, fostering internal peace.

Moreover, the importance of a supportive social network can't be overstated. Interacting with loved ones, joining support groups, or simply engaging in social activities can offer emotional ballast during challenging times.

As we progress through this chapter, it becomes evident that treating mental health is both an art and a science. The amalgamation of evidence-based practices with individualized care often leads to the most promising outcomes.

Chapter 6: Substance Abuse and Mental Health

In the tapestry of human experience, the relationship between mental health and substance use is intricate. For some, substances offer an escape or a way to cope with mental anguish; for others, their excessive consumption might instigate or exacerbate mental health problems. The two frequently interact in a cyclical manner, each influencing the other, underscoring the importance of understanding their interrelation.

Alcohol

Alcohol, a socially sanctioned substance, has, for centuries, been a fixture in many cultural rituals and gatherings. When consumed in moderation, it can foster sociability and relaxation. However, its overindulgence or dependence has profound implications on mental health.

Chronic heavy drinking is associated with a range of mental health problems. Depression, anxiety, and sleep disturbances are common among heavy drinkers. The euphoria of the first drink can quickly give way to feelings of sadness, irritability, and paranoia. Furthermore, alcohol's depressant effects on the central nervous system can dampen the very emotions one might be trying to elevate.

Recovery from alcohol addiction isn't just about stopping consumption. It's about understanding the underlying emotional triggers that lead to excessive drinking and addressing coexisting mental health issues.

Substance Abuse and Mental Health

Drugs

From the allure of hallucinogens to the euphoria offered by stimulants, drugs encompass a broad category, each with distinct psychological effects. The recreational use of drugs, whether it's ecstasy at a music festival or cocaine at a high-end party, might seem harmless initially. However, chronic use can pave the way for a host of mental health challenges.

Stimulants, like cocaine and methamphetamine, might give an initial rush of energy and pleasure but can also lead to anxiety, paranoia, and aggressive behavior. On the other end, depressants can lead to feelings of relaxation but can also deepen feelings of sadness or lethargy. Long-term drug use can disrupt the brain's reward system, making it harder for individuals to feel pleasure without the substance, leading to depression

Cannabis

Cannabis, in its various forms, has been a topic of global conversation. With changing legal stances and its therapeutic use, it's essential to understand its complex relationship with mental health.

While many tout cannabis for its relaxation properties and potential therapeutic benefits for conditions like chronic pain or even anxiety, it's not devoid of concerns. High doses or early and frequent use during teenage years can be associated with an increased risk of depression in adulthood. There's also a well-established connection between cannabis and psychosis, especially for those with a predisposition to such conditions.

Substance Abuse and Mental Health

Opioids

The opioid crisis has brought to the fore the devastating impact of these potent drugs. Derived from the poppy plant, opioids can offer profound pain relief. However, their overuse can be fatal.

Mentally, opioids can induce a state of euphoria, but they also suppress the respiratory center in the brain. Over time, individuals may require more of the drug to achieve the same effect, leading to a dangerous spiral of increasing dosage. Chronic use can give rise to feelings of anxiety, paranoia, and depression. The dependence on opioids can become the central focus of an individual's life, sidelining their relationships, career, and even their health.

The intertwining of substance use with mental health cannot be overstressed. Recognizing the signs, understanding the triggers, and seeking timely intervention can be life-changing, if not life-saving. As we explore further, the importance of comprehensive care that addresses both substance use and underlying mental health issues becomes evident. This holistic approach is not just about healing the mind and body but rejuvenating the spirit.

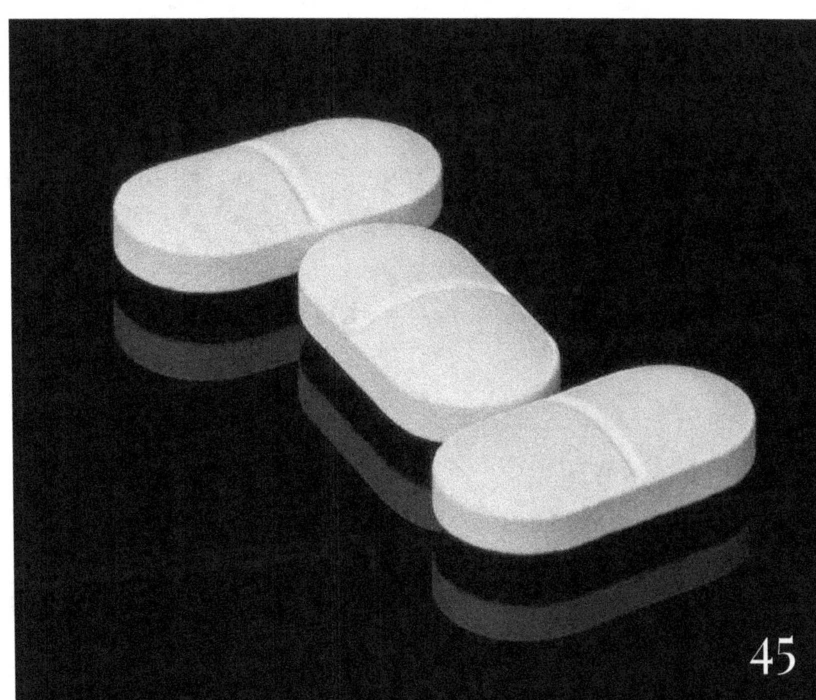

Substance Abuse and Mental Health

Recognizing the intertwined nature of substance use and mental health is essential. Timely interventions can be transformative and even lifesaving. Comprehensive care addressing both substance misuse and coexisting mental health issues can rejuvenate the individual holistically.

Understanding Substance Use Disorder (SUD)

Substance Use Disorder (SUD) is a multifaceted condition characterized by uncontrolled substance consumption despite adverse consequences. SUD can lead to impaired daily functioning and relentless substance cravings, even in the face of known risks.

Changes in brain function and structure underpin SUD, causing cravings, personality shifts, and altered behaviors. Persistent substance use can lead to lasting changes in brain function, affecting judgment, decision-making, and behavior.

Tolerance, a hallmark of SUD, signifies the need for increasing substance amounts to achieve the same effects.

Several factors influence substance use:

1. Pleasure or "high"

2. Coping mechanism to relieve stress or numb emotions.

3. Performance or cognitive enhancement.

4. Curiosity, peer pressure, or experimentation.

Substance Abuse and Mental Health

Beyond substances, behavioral addictions, such as gambling, can develop. Such disorders can lead to interpersonal strife and are significant contributors to preventable illnesses and deaths.

Treatment for Substance Use Disorder

The first step toward treatment is recognizing the problem. Medical professionals can assess and diagnose SUD. Tailored treatment, addressing both substance misuse and coexisting medical or psychiatric issues, is most effective.

Medications can manage drug cravings, withdrawal symptoms, and prevent relapse. Psychotherapy helps individuals understand their behavior, boosts self-esteem, and addresses other psychiatric issues.

Potential treatment modalities include:

- Detoxification in hospitals.

- Therapeutic communities or sober houses.

- Outpatient medication and psychotherapy.

- Intensive outpatient programs.

- Residential treatment or "rehab".

- Mutual-aid groups like AA or NA.

- Family-inclusive self-help groups like Al-Anon or Nar-Anon.

Substance Abuse and Mental Health

The National Institute on Drug Abuse proposes 13 principles for effective drug addiction treatment, highlighting the importance of comprehensive, individualized care.

Supporting Someone with SUD:

• Educate yourself about addiction.

• Express concern and offer help.

• Encourage professional treatment.

• Understand that recovery is an ongoing process.

• Avoid moralizing, covering up for them, or assuming their responsibilities.

• Engage in discussions when they're sober.

• Don't feel responsible for their choices.

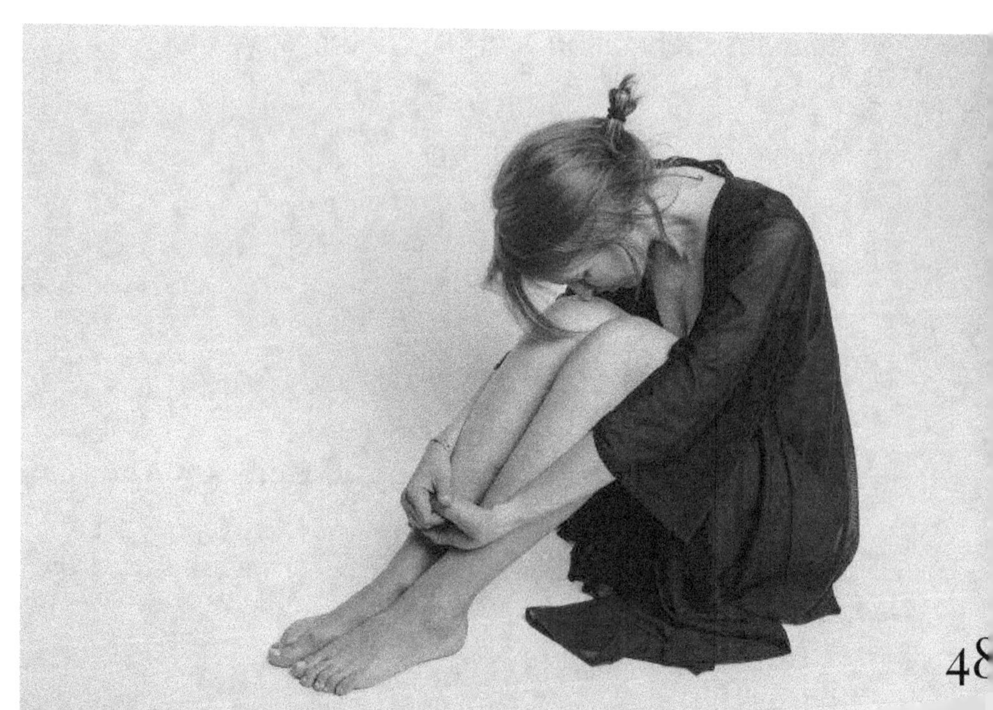

Chapter 7: Technology and Mental Health

In the unfolding narrative of human history, the digital revolution stands as one of the most transformative epochs. From the moment we wake up to the lullaby of nighttime, technology has woven itself into every fabric of our lives. While it offers an array of conveniences, its implications for mental health are a kaleidoscope of benefits and challenges. In this chapter, we'll delve deep into some of the most poignant intersections of technology and our mental well-being.

AI Relationships

Once a theme restricted to the domain of sci-fi novels and movies, Artificial Intelligence (AI) has started making waves in the realm of human relationships. From AI-driven chatbots providing company to digital companions simulating friendship or even romance, the boundary between human and digital interaction is increasingly getting blurred.

On one hand, AI relationships offer a solace of sorts to those feeling isolated or those who struggle with human interactions. For some, the predictable nature of AI can be comforting, free from the complexities and unpredictabilities of human emotion.

However, over-reliance on AI for emotional support can also raise concerns. By sidestepping human interaction, one might miss out on the richness, depth, and growth that come from navigating the intricacies of human relationships. Moreover, AI, for all its advancements, lacks genuine empathy and the human touch, crucial for deep emotional healing and connection.

Technology and Mental Health

Screen Time Effects

The glow of screens, be it smartphones, tablets, or laptops, has become a near-constant presence. With a world of information and entertainment at our fingertips, the advantages are manifold. But, the effects of prolonged screen time on mental health can't be brushed aside.

Excessive screen time has been linked to disruptions in sleep patterns, primarily if used before bedtime. The blue light emitted can interfere with the production of melatonin, a hormone vital for sleep. Beyond physical effects, being perennially plugged in can lead to feelings of anxiety, depression, and social isolation. The world portrayed online, often curated and idealized, can skew perceptions, leading to feelings of inadequacy or FOMO (Fear of Missing Out).

The paradox of being more connected yet feeling more isolated in the digital age is a real challenge. Finding a balance, setting boundaries, and practicing digital detox can play a significant role in ensuring that technology serves us, not the other way around.

Technology and Mental Health

Teletherapy

Emerging as a beacon of hope and convenience in the vast landscape of mental health treatments, teletherapy has revolutionized access to therapeutic services. Using technology to connect therapists and clients, it breaks down geographical barriers, allowing individuals to seek help from the comfort of their homes.

The benefits are multifaceted. For those residing in remote areas or those with mobility challenges, teletherapy can be a godsend. The comfort of being in a familiar environment can also make therapy more accessible for those hesitant to seek help.

However, it's not without its set of challenges. Technical glitches, concerns about data privacy, and the lack of physical presence can sometimes impede the therapeutic process. For some, the tactile experience of being in the same room, the nuances of body language, and the tangible presence of another human are irreplaceable.

As technology continues to chart its course, its impact on mental health will remain a topic of fervent discussion and research. Embracing its benefits while being cognizant of its potential pitfalls will be the key. After all, in this dance between the digital and the human, it's essential to ensure that technology augments our humanity, not diminishes it.

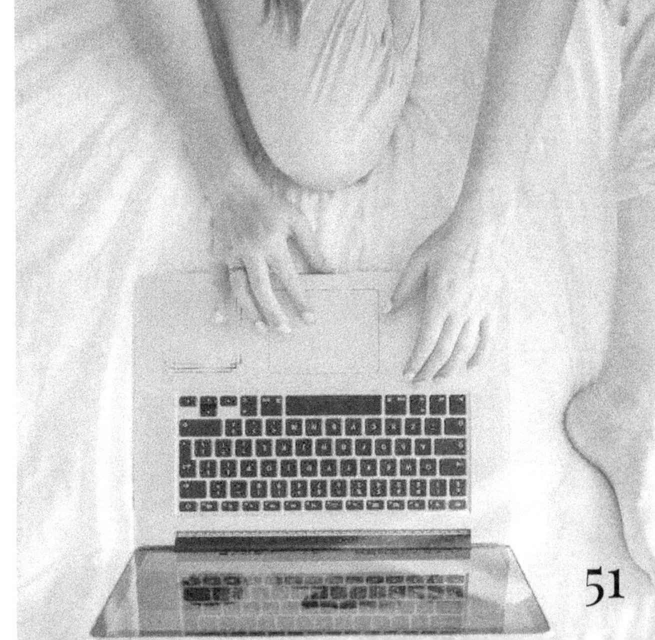

Chapter 8: What is Mental Health?

Mental health, an integral facet of our holistic well-being, encompasses our ability to navigate life's challenges, recognize our strengths, contribute to our communities, and nurture harmonious existence. It forms the bedrock of our decision-making, relationships, and the very fabric of the world we inhabit. Beyond the realm of mental disorders, mental health spans a diverse spectrum, varying individually, characterized by a wide array of challenges and distress, which in turn can lead to a myriad of social and clinical outcomes.

The concept underlying mental health is its fluid nature, existing on a continuum influenced by a multitude of factors. These factors, ranging from individual attributes to societal dynamics and structural intricacies, weave together to either fortify or undermine our mental well-being.

Within the intricate web of mental health, both protective and risk factors play a pivotal role in shaping our psychological landscape. Individual elements, such as genetics and emotional intelligence, interlace with external influences like socioeconomic disparities, violence, and inequality. These factors hold the power to shield us from adversities or expose us to challenges, particularly during crucial developmental phases such as early childhood.

Resilience, cultivated through attributes like social support, emotional skills, quality education, and positive interactions, acts as a buffer against the potential negative impacts of life's stressors and hurdles. These protective elements work to mitigate the effects of challenges we encounter. However, it's crucial to acknowledge that mental health is a dynamic construct, shaped by a tapestry of influences, some within our control and others beyond it.

What is Mental Health?

At the heart of enhancing individual and collective well-being lies mental health promotion and prevention. These strategies are rooted in a profound comprehension of the determinants that contribute to mental health. Their aim is to mitigate risks, strengthen resilience, and foster environments that nurture mental well-being. The scope of these initiatives extends far beyond healthcare, necessitating collaboration across diverse sectors such as education, labor, justice, transportation, environment, housing, and welfare.

This calls for a holistic approach that transcends the confines of traditional healthcare. Suicide prevention and interventions to foster mental health among children, adolescents, and the workforce are vital aspects of this approach. Strategies encompass limiting access to harmful means, cultivating nurturing environments, promoting emotional learning, and integrating mental health services with general healthcare. These strategies are versatile and adaptable, catering to various populations and contexts.

Embedded within the spectrum of mental health care and treatment is community-based care. This model, a departure from institutionalized approaches, focuses on accessibility, human rights, and heightened recovery outcomes. Through an interconnected network of services including general healthcare, community mental health centers, psychosocial rehabilitation, peer support services, and care offered in diverse settings, this approach aims to provide comprehensive and holistic mental health support.

Addressing the treatment gap for common mental health conditions, like depression and anxiety, requires innovative approaches. Digital self-help, non-specialist psychological counseling, and diverse modes of support hold potential to bridge this gap and make mental health care more accessible.

What is Mental Health?

To address the fundamental question "What is mental health?" is to weave a narrative entwining personal experiences, societal influences, and structural determinants. This journey goes beyond individual boundaries, shaping our thoughts, emotions, and interactions. Understanding mental health surpasses words on a page; it's recognizing its profound relevance in our lives and collectively striving to foster a world where emotional well-being flourishes.

To answer the question of what mental health is, we turn to the realm of mental illness. Mental illnesses are medical conditions that disrupt a person's thinking, feeling, mood, ability to relate to others, and daily functioning. Just as diabetes is a disorder of the pancreas, mental illnesses are medical conditions that often result in a diminished capacity for coping with the ordinary demands of life.

Serious mental health conditions include major depression, schizophrenia, bipolar disorder, obsessive-compulsive disorder (OCD), anxiety disorders, post-traumatic stress disorder (PTSD), and borderline personality disorder. The positive news is that recovery is possible.

Mental illnesses can impact individuals regardless of age, race, religion, or income. Mental illnesses are not a result of personal weakness, character deficits, or poor upbringing. Mental health conditions cannot be overcome through sheer willpower and are not indicative of a person's character or intelligence; they are treatable. Most individuals diagnosed with serious mental illnesses can find relief from their symptoms by actively participating in an individualized treatment plan.

In addition to medication treatment, psychosocial treatment like cognitive-behavioral therapy, interpersonal therapy, peer support groups, and other community services can play a pivotal role. The U.S. Surgeon General has reported that 10 percent of children and adolescents in the United States suffer from serious emotional and mental disorders that significantly impair their daily lives at home, in school, and with peers.

What is Mental Health?

The World Health Organization has revealed that four of the ten leading causes of disability in the US and other developed countries are mental disorders. In 2021, Major Depressive illness became the leading cause of disability worldwide for women and children.

Mental illnesses often strike individuals during their prime years, particularly during adolescence and young adulthood. However, all age groups are susceptible, with the young and elderly being particularly vulnerable.

Left untreated, the consequences of mental illness for both individuals and society can be staggering. Untreated mental health conditions can result in unnecessary disability, unemployment, substance abuse, homelessness, improper incarceration, and even suicide, leading to a diminished quality of life. The economic toll of untreated mental illness exceeds 100 billion dollars each year in the United States.

Today, the best treatments for serious mental illnesses are highly effective, with between 70 and 90 percent of individuals experiencing a significant reduction in symptoms and an improved quality of life through a combination of pharmacological and psychosocial treatments and supports.

With the right medication and a variety of services tailored to individual needs, most people living with serious mental illnesses can significantly reduce the impact of their conditions and find a sense of achievement and independence. A fundamental concept is to develop strategies to manage the illness process.

Early identification and treatment are of paramount importance; by ensuring access to effective treatment and recovery supports, the recovery process can be accelerated and further harm related to the course of the illness can be minimized.

What is Mental Health?

Stigma erodes the confidence that mental disorders are real and treatable health conditions. Our society has allowed stigma and an unwarranted sense of hopelessness to erect barriers to effective treatment and recovery. The time has come to dismantle these barriers and cultivate a more inclusive and compassionate approach to mental health and well-being.

In conclusion, understanding mental health requires delving into the intricate interplay of individual attributes, societal dynamics, and structural determinants. It's a journey that extends beyond personal boundaries, influencing our thoughts, emotions, and interactions. Recognizing mental health's significance isn't confined to mere words; it's about acknowledging its profound impact on our lives and working together to create a world where emotional well-being thrives. To answer the question of what mental health is, we delve into the realm of mental illnesses, medical conditions that disrupt various aspects of life, but hold the promise of recovery and resilience.

Chapter 9: Socio-cultural Factors Impacting Mental Health

Mental health, while deeply personal, is also intricately woven into the societal and cultural fabric that envelops us. Every society possesses its unique set of cultural and social norms, an intergenerational inheritance of learned behaviors and beliefs that define distinct social groups. These cultural underpinnings are molded by shared experiences and leave an indelible mark on people's way of life and belief systems. Within this complex tapestry, ethnicity, race, religion, and family values stand as influences that collectively forge culture.

Socio-cultural Factors Impacting Mental Health

The experience and manifestation of mental illness are far from immune to these cultural currents. Indeed, an individual's social and cultural background plays a pivotal role in determining how mental illness is expressed. It shapes the language with which individuals communicate their symptoms, influences their comprehension of their condition, dictates the coping mechanisms they adopt, and even steers the type of interventions they pursue.

Nevertheless, it's imperative to tread cautiously when discussing cultural beliefs and customs. Engaging in broad generalizations risks the perilous terrain of stereotyping, a pitfall that overlooks the rich diversity within any racial, ethnic, or cultural group. The reality is that factors such as age, income, health status, and social class meld with cultural backgrounds to uniquely color each individual's interpretation.

Within the United Kingdom's mental health care system, the foundation is firmly rooted in Western medicine and research. This framework places a premium on empirical evidence, viewing mental illness as a product of physiological or biological causes susceptible to medical intervention. However, the resonance of this model predominantly echoes within those who possess knowledge of and faith in modern medicine, leading them to seek consultation from psychiatrists or psychological practitioners.

The intricate dance between culture and mental health is evident in studies that reveal how culture influences patient-clinician interactions. For instance, research has unveiled that Asian patients tend to articulate physical symptoms more frequently than emotional ones. This divergence in symptom presentation can profoundly sway the diagnosis and subsequent treatment plan.

Socio-cultural Factors Impacting Mental Health

Moreover, culture extends its hand to the very meaning that individuals ascribe to their mental health condition. This framework of interpretation shapes whether a patient perceives their condition as tangible or elusive, mental or physiological, deserving sympathy or scrutiny.

Intriguingly, culture exerts its influence on the very act of seeking treatment. It lays out the pathways individuals traverse when seeking support, channeling them toward family, community, and specific resources, thereby influencing not just how they seek help but where.

Yet, the outcomes of these cultural influences are not confined to the realm of the positive. In some cases, the consequences can be grave, leading to severe negative implications. There are instances where individuals, deprived of adequate treatment and support due to cultural constraints, turn to suicide as a distressing alternative.

Delving into historical contexts, the origins of mental illness explanations trace back to attributions of supernatural forces or possession by malevolent spirits that disrupt the human psyche. Astonishingly, traces of these beliefs endure in modern society. Various theories surrounding the etiology of mental illness have been postulated, including the supernatural theory, shock theory, and biochemical theory. The supernatural theory propounds the notion that malevolent spirits inhabit individuals, engendering a shift in their psychological makeup.

The spectrum of belief systems in relation to mental health is far from monolithic. Some individuals adhering to supernatural explanations for mental illness gravitate towards places of worship and faith healers, circumventing conventional psychiatric or psychological treatment. Fascinatingly, there are those who integrate traditional and medical models of mental illness.

Socio-cultural Factors Impacting Mental Health

Culture extends its grasp to coping mechanisms as well. For instance, African communities frequently adopt autonomous strategies in managing adversities. In their approach to mental health challenges and the vicissitudes of life, spirituality emerges as a crucial wellspring.

Though the realm of culture's impact on mental health remains an arena ripe for deeper exploration, existing research underscores noteworthy trends. Ethnic minority groups often display a tendency to delay seeking mental health treatment and, instead, favor informal sources like clergy, traditional healers, family, and friends. For instance, Africans often lean on religious ministers, who multifariously assume roles related to mental health, ranging from counseling and diagnostics to referrals.

In closing, the chapter of socio-cultural factors intertwining with mental health is rife with complexities and nuances. While some cultural practices may act as impediments to effective mental illness management, they simultaneously serve as signposts directing us toward the creation of innovative frameworks tailored to culturally diverse populations. Culture exerts a profound influence across various aspects of mental health, including the construction of health perceptions, patterns of seeking treatment, and strategies for coping.

This intricate interplay beckons us to abandon the notion that a standardized approach to mental health care can adequately address the needs of culturally diverse communities. Instead, it underscores the imperative of cultivating transcultural training for mental health professionals and policymakers. Institutions must recognize that integrating Western health concepts with constructive traditional and community-based strategies is pivotal. In this endeavor, it's imperative to acknowledge that every individual's journey and cultural context is uniquely different, requiring a bespoke approach to achieving holistic mental equilibrium.

Chapter 10: Future Perspectives

In the realm of mental health care and data collection, technology has ushered in a new era, reshaping access to help, progress monitoring, and comprehension of mental well-being. The proliferation of mobile devices such as cell phones, smartphones, and tablets has forged novel pathways for the public, healthcare providers, and researchers to engage with mental health.

The simplicity and efficacy of mobile mental health support are exemplified by resources like Suicide and Crisis Lifeline. Accessible through phones and computers, this lifeline offers immediate assistance through calls, texts, or chats, serving as a lifeline in critical moments.

On the technological forefront, sophisticated apps tailored for smartphones and tablets embody the potential for revolutionary change. These apps harness the power of device sensors to capture data on users' typical behavioral patterns. When deviations are detected, these apps can preemptively signal the need for help, averting crises before they unfold.

The gamut of apps extends beyond crisis intervention. Some apps are designed to enhance memory or cognitive skills, while others facilitate connections with peer counselors or healthcare professionals. The burgeoning landscape of mental health apps is burgeoning, with thousands available in iTunes and Android app stores. However, amid this digital bloom, an environment of uncertainty prevails. The scarcity of industry regulations and data on app efficacy raises questions about trustworthiness.

Before delving into the trajectory of scientific advancement and its implications, it is prudent to assess the pros and cons of expanding mental health treatment and research into the realm of technology. The ever-deepening insights into the intricacies of the human brain are concurrently elevating our comprehension of mental illnesses.

Chapter 10: Future Perspectives

Modern technology empowers medical researchers to dissect individuals' DNA, identifying specific genes correlated with distinct mental disorders. Hormonal signals and brain scans supplement these genetic analyses, unraveling anomalies and nuances. This growing body of knowledge empowers psychiatrists and doctors to decipher the etiology of mental illnesses and prescribe tailored treatment strategies. This precision enables swift and widespread diagnosis, making it feasible for those traditionally excluded from therapy due to lack of access or financial constraints to receive accurate diagnosis and targeted treatment.

Looking to the future, psychiatry appears destined to be intrinsically personalized. Patients might not even need to leave their homes to access care. Virtual therapy platforms already orchestrate online sessions, extending therapeutic support to individuals who may otherwise remain untreated. This innovation addresses barriers faced by rural communities and individuals who feel apprehensive about visiting a therapist's office. The cost-effectiveness of these virtual interventions is augmented by the increasing coverage by insurance policies. Moreover, the proliferation of high-speed internet and advanced camera technology ensures that virtual sessions can rival the effectiveness of in-person consultations.

In tandem with technological advances, public perceptions surrounding mental health are undergoing a transformation. The burgeoning number of public figures candidly discussing their battles with mental illness is chipping away at the stigma of seeking treatment. As societal discourse broadens and diversifies, the acknowledgment that mental health challenges are prevalent and amenable to treatment is gaining ground.

While the marriage of technology and mental health offers promising horizons, it also begets a series of ethical considerations. Data privacy, security, and the need for rigorous scientific validation pose complex challenges. Moreover, the digital divide, which disproportionately affects marginalized communities, must be addressed to ensure equitable access to these revolutionary advancements.

Future Perspectives

Modern technology empowers medical researchers to dissect individuals' DNA, identifying specific genes correlated with distinct mental disorders. Hormonal signals and brain scans supplement these genetic analyses, unraveling anomalies and nuances. This growing body of knowledge empowers psychiatrists and doctors to decipher the etiology of mental illnesses and prescribe tailored treatment strategies. This precision enables swift and widespread diagnosis, making it feasible for those traditionally excluded from therapy due to lack of access or financial constraints to receive accurate diagnosis and targeted treatment.

Looking to the future, psychiatry appears destined to be intrinsically personalized. Patients might not even need to leave their homes to access care. Virtual therapy platforms already orchestrate online sessions, extending therapeutic support to individuals who may otherwise remain untreated. This innovation addresses barriers faced by rural communities and individuals who feel apprehensive about visiting a therapist's office. The cost-effectiveness of these virtual interventions is augmented by the increasing coverage by insurance policies. Moreover, the proliferation of high-speed internet and advanced camera technology ensures that virtual sessions can rival the effectiveness of in-person consultations.

In tandem with technological advances, public perceptions surrounding mental health are undergoing a transformation. The burgeoning number of public figures candidly discussing their battles with mental illness is chipping away at the stigma of seeking treatment. As societal discourse broadens and diversifies, the acknowledgment that mental health challenges are prevalent and amenable to treatment is gaining ground.

Future Perspectives

While the marriage of technology and mental health offers promising horizons, it also begets a series of ethical considerations. Data privacy, security, and the need for rigorous scientific validation pose complex challenges. Moreover, the digital divide, which disproportionately affects marginalized communities, must be addressed to ensure equitable access to these revolutionary advancements.

As we peer into the future, the convergence of technology, research, and societal change holds the potential to redefine mental health care. A landscape where personalized treatments are accessible at one's fingertips is not merely a dream, but an evolving reality that promises to rewrite the script of mental well-being for generations to come.

Chapter 11: Conclusion

As we draw the threads of this exploration to a close, it becomes vividly apparent that understanding mental health is a dynamic journey through various dimensions. From debunking misconceptions to unveiling the complexities of disorders, from understanding symptoms to exploring treatment avenues, from scrutinizing the interplay of substance abuse to envisioning the role of technology, from probing the core essence of mental health to delving into socio-cultural influences, and finally, peering into the horizon of future perspectives – each chapter has unfurled a layer of understanding, contributing to a comprehensive tapestry of knowledge.

In the realm of misconception, we dissected the webs of fallacies that often obscure our perception of mental health, replacing them with clarity and empathy. We unraveled deeply rooted myths that hinder understanding and foster stigma, striving to create a canvas where accurate information and open conversations can flourish.

Transitioning into the chapters of mental health disorders, we ventured into the intricate labyrinths of conditions that challenge our well-being. From the ubiquitous presence of anxiety and depression to the intricate landscape of bipolar disorder and schizophrenia, each disorder was dissected to reveal its unique manifestations, root causes, and potential interventions. We illuminated the paths to identification, drawing attention to the subtleties that often elude detection and emphasizing the significance of early recognition for effective treatment.

The expedition into treatments illuminated a landscape of hope and possibilities. From the holistic approaches of psychotherapy to the targeted precision of medication, we acknowledged that treatment isn't a one-size-fits-all solution. The intersection of science, psychology, and empathy was unveiled as the cornerstone of successful intervention, emphasizing that recovery is not only possible but attainable through a collaborative effort.

Conclusion

The nexus between substance abuse and mental health revealed a complex interplay that often exacerbates both realms. We dissected the interconnectedness, recognizing the crucial role of integrated interventions that address the dual challenges. This chapter served as a poignant reminder that understanding mental health requires acknowledging its interconnectedness with various facets of our lives.

In a world driven by technology, we ventured into a chapter that explored the intersection of innovation and mental health. We discovered the transformative potential of mobile mental health support, virtual therapy, and advanced applications. However, we also navigated through the uncharted territories of privacy concerns and efficacy challenges, recognizing the necessity for careful navigation through this evolving landscape.

As we plunged into the heart of the question "What is mental health?" we unearthed its multidimensional essence. From the intricate symphony of biological factors to the intricate dance of emotions, from the pivotal significance of relationships to the influence of culture and society, we comprehended that mental health is far from a singular definition. It is the fusion of these influences that shapes our mental landscape, transcending mere absence of illness to encompass a dynamic state of well-being.

The socio-cultural dimension emerged as a profound tapestry within the mental health discourse. We navigated through the influences of culture, ethnicity, race, and societal norms, recognizing how these factors impact the experience, perception, and response to mental health challenges. The significance of cultural competence and the imperative of dismantling stigma reverberated as essential pillars in fostering an inclusive understanding of mental well-being.

Conclusion

Peering into the horizon, we glimpsed the landscape of future perspectives. The convergence of technology and mental health promises a revolution in access and intervention. The potential for personalized treatment plans, virtual therapy, and advanced applications holds the promise of transforming the mental health care landscape. However, this newfound frontier comes with its own challenges, underscoring the need for careful consideration and ethical navigation.

As these chapters interweave, the sum emerges as far greater than its parts. Mental health isn't merely an individual affair; it's an intricate tapestry woven from the threads of biology, psychology, relationships, culture, society, and technology. It's a journey that traverses misconceptions, embraces diversity, and envisions a future of healing. It's a journey that demands awareness, compassion, and an unwavering commitment to eradicating stigma.

In conclusion, our exploration isn't confined to these chapters alone; it echoes beyond, transcending boundaries. The mosaic of mental health is ever-evolving, dynamic, and deeply intertwined with the human experience. It calls for a collective effort, where individuals, families, communities, and societies weave threads of understanding, empathy, and hope into its fabric. As we step away from these pages, may we carry forward the awareness that mental health isn't a destination but a journey, a journey marked by resilience, compassion, and the ever-present prospect of growth.

So, as we move forward, let us be catalysts for change. Let us be champions of understanding, advocates of empathy, and ambassadors of mental well-being. Let the tapestry we've woven through these chapters be a reminder that mental health is a shared journey, a journey that harmonizes our biological, emotional, relational, and societal dimensions into a symphony of resilience and hope.

The End.

References

1. American Psychiatric Association (APA) - **www.psychiatry.org**

2. National Institute of Mental Health (NIMH) - **www.nimh.nih.gov**

3. World Health Organization (WHO) - **www.who.int/mental_health**

4. Mental Health America (MHA) - **www.mhanational.org**

5. National Alliance on Mental Illness (NAMI) - **www.nami.org**

6. Mayo Clinic - **www.mayoclinic.org**

7. Centers for Disease Control and Prevention (CDC) - **www.cdc.gov/mentalhealth**

8. Harvard Health Publishing - **www.health.harvard.edu/topics/mental-health**

9. National Institute on Drug Abuse (NIDA) - **www.drugabuse.gov**

10. Substance Abuse and Mental Health Services Administration (SAMHSA) - **www.samhsa.gov**

Copyright © 2023 by Yousef Naser

All rights reserved. No part of this publication may be reproduced, distributed, or transmitted in any form or by any means, including photocopying, recording, or other electronic or mechanical methods, without the prior written permission of the publisher, except in the case of brief quotations embodied in critical reviews and certain other noncommercial uses permitted by copyright law.

www.ingramcontent.com/pod-product-compliance
Lightning Source LLC
Chambersburg PA
CBHW060126120726
48003CB00009B/2784